vērtigo

Of Love & Letting Go

Analog de Lēon

Andrews McMeel
PUBLISHING®

Andrews McMeel Publishing
a division of Andrews McMeel Universal
1130 Walnut Street, Kansas City, Missouri 64106

www.andrewsmcmeel.com
www.goingvertigo.com

17 18 19 20 21 RR2 10 9 8 7 6 5 4 3 2 1

ISBN: 978-1-4494-8775-1

Library of Congress Control Number: 2017936775
)

Editor: Patty Rice
Art Director: Holly Swayne
Illustrators: Amy Purifoy, Analog de Léon
Production Editor: Amy Strassner
Creative Editors: Fiorella Giordano, Gabriel Sage
Production Manager: Cliff Koehler

Attention: Schools and Businesses
Andrews McMeel books are available at quantity discounts with
bulk purchase for educational, business, or sales promotional use.
For information, please e-mail the Andrews McMeel Publishing
Special Sales Department: specialsales@amuniversal.com.

O'Found

For Amy

There is a secret
written in the stars and in the mountains.

Learn clues to the secret
and take an interactive journey
through the rabbit hole.

goingvertigo.com/secret

Listen while you read.

goingvertigo.com/playlist

me • *vērtigo* • her

"When love awakens in your life, in the night of your heart, it is like the dawn breaking within you."

—JOHN O'DONOHUE

John O'Donohue thought a flickering candle in a dark room to be the most beautiful scene the universe could possess. This image never left me. When I first imagined the mysterious candle, I saw *her*. My *Anam Cara*. She is an idea that could launch a thousand ships.

Later I learned that a candle was the key that let us map our universe.

A professor at a university once asked several of his students to row out in boats onto a pond. He gave each of them a candle and positioned their boats near to far every few feet. That night they learned that light has a brightness and a color that determines how close or far away it is from the source. Scientists used this new idea to calculate the size of our universe and to determine exactly where each star is in the cosmic sea, and it taught me a deep mystery about myself and my relationship with the universe.

Today, the unit for the brightness or dimness of a star is a *candle*. It measures a star's luminosity. This new science taught us that a star moving away from the Earth appears *red* and when moving toward us, a star cools to *blue*.

She must be one million *red candles*.

It is remarkable how a lesson hidden in a simple candle can catalyze a massive change in our perspective and relationship to the universe. We are no longer lost. We have a location in the vastness.

These days when I imagine a candle dancing on a cave wall, I see a deep mystery. A foreign belly dancer unfolding on the rocks, serving my fascination with full awareness. I can't look away. I see God in the flickering light.

Powerful ideas and symbols live and evolve in us like the taste of wine. The more complex an idea, the more layers of the onion. Like hieroglyphics, great symbols require interpretation and deep inspection through a *blue* filter to unearth their light. We have to seek truth. It never leaves us, but it waits for us to stop running and draw closer to it.

Vertigo is presented here in three parts, though it is really just one work in three. At its root, *Vertigo* attempts to convey a sense of wholeness. It has been broken up into individual stanzas that can be read consecutively, but *Vertigo* is really just one epic style poem.

The illustrations tell the story of a turbulent journey from separation to oneness, that has taken me more than a decade to distill, and it also chronicles two weeks of my life one February when the dawn broke within me. It's interesting how the phases of the moon leave a fingerprint in time, a unique record for each day in the sky.

Vertigo was inspired by O'Donohue's curious candle and St. Simeon Stylites, a Syrian who lived for several years on a small platform atop a pillar—the final stand against a great tide of darkness. It is a story that has been stirring in me for more than a decade. A map for a lost generation of anxious people holding on for life as the train of progress careens violently forward into midnight.

This brave new age is trying desperately to convince us that we are digital, that our humanity is not of the earth but of the air, of the Wi-Fi and the radio waves, of the 4Gs and the AIs. If you take anything from this book, I hope it is a deeper presence with yourself and the people in your life. When I learned to unplug and be present, I was taught a great secret. My greatest hope is that *Vertigo* encourages you to seek out the white space in your days, those moments of clarity with the wind that restore your soul and guide your steps.

Vertigo is about the relationship between love and light, loss and darkness, our humanity and the infinite. These relationships don't seem definable as an intellectual process, as if the fabric that connects them is encrypted and can't be accessed or understood without examining it with some higher human function.

Vertigo is a book about letting go.

"Each mind fabricates itself.
We sense its limits for we have made them."

—RILKE

The stars crossed
when they first said
hello.

vērtigo in three

rooftop of the world

When a mountain
begins to smoke,
rest assured an ancient fire
has begun a holy pilgrimage
to the surface.

I step out, curious,
onto the rooftop of the world.
My compass spins violently
along with my vision.

I can see her reflecting like the moon
between hurried breaths and blinks.

She followed me
to the top.

I go stand higher
to see the full picture.
I pause until I am aware of myself,
marinate in the moment
and find a dwelling in the silence
above the *n o i s e.*

I am the narrow gate
that leads inward
and the tower
standing beacon in separation.

I reach in and unearth
the false agreements
that have walled up
my secret places for so long,
then I step back from the ledge.

Change begins with one step.

I climbed
to the edge of terror
to free myself.

How did she
find me here?

I close my eyes.
I draw into the stillness of secret.
Into the truth of this eternal moment.
This curious *boundless* flame.

I remember *blue* and nothing,
a heavenly distortion.
My roots in whirling wind.

Vertigo is *letting go*.

vērtigo at midnight

I follow a brick road for days
until I reach her hollow courts.
It seems the masons
who built her kingdom
erected the castle walls
with the same stones
that paved her vulnerability.

14FEB . 23h53m01s

There's something about
her high places.
I learn to lift scaffolds
to scale her walls,
but how high are her arches
that hands and words
are not enough to reach her?

Hands and words
are feeble tools for feeble bodies,
fire does not need such institutions.

I once heard the most beautiful
of all creations lives in the shadow
of a candle on a cave wall.

It moves across the stone
with the pulse of some great ocean,
like a belly dancer's hips
in sways of truth in motion.

I can see her reflecting
in the cave light.

She is the sea,
wild and free.

I know I could never
fully explore her expanse
and will most certainly
become lost in her waves forever,
yet with a torn sail and a smile,
I set sail anyhow.

Like a cathedral,

she coaxes my light into permanence

in the inner courts of her soul.

No mortal man

has ever unveiled her,

but I press on

as she gives me passage.

Like a god,
I can see all her thoughts
and am privy to the makeup
of each fiber that holds her together.

Like a priest,
she gives me absolution,
while the light unfolds into flames
in the crevices of her skin.

If God is love,
she must be an ancient temple.

"Sing in me, Muse."

15FEB

She
is
my
secret
place—
where my light begins.

Until her
there was no forever.
A fleeting light—
I chase her in spirals
like the Ouroboros.

She flees from me like Orion,
a great huntress afraid of scorpions.

Is life not an endless ring of motion?
Is love not an endless ring of devotion?

What if all there ever was with us
was only meant to live
for one brief but perfect moment,
like a short masterpiece on repeat
unfolding again and again
in frames that have long since had their end?

I reach out
as a chasm grows between us,
but she is already gone—
her heart a restless vessel
that has long ago set course
for some distant ardent shore.

I changed everything for her.

I have nothing in common
with the man I have become.

She is betrothed to another.
The muse is not always
the b e l o v e d.

There is now only
a hollow ringing in our ears
that demands
one of us bring the noise to silence,
but I could never leave.

She will have to *break me.*

— tidal waves —

I am thrown powerless.
I drown in defiance like Odysseus,
the last soul alive on a great Titanic.

16FEB

♍ ●

She says goodbye.
I become an island.
An ocean swells between us.

I drink from the pool of memory,
so I will remember . . .

— *supernova in paradise* —

No one tells you
when you fall in love with a star,
one day it might burn out
and leave behind a black hole.

She is gone—
her castle cold.
Her silence sounds like sirens
as my bones grow old.

— *the arrow of time moves forward* —

I never let go.

Even now it feels like any day
a polar shift
could violently reshape the landscape,
melt the glaciers
and bring back spring to this cold place.

I've been sleeping in
as long as I can these days,
for even though she is missing
from my sheets when I wake,
I have hidden her
beneath the *silk of my dreams.*

Her light is too bright.
I see only *yellow*.

17FEB

ⅶ 🌑

Like waiting for a ship to arrive,
I can see her on the horizon,
but I can't reach her.

I imagine her returning
on the great ocean of time.

I *wait* for her to receive me
and become a
                    m a r t y r
to my own intentions.

There are fewer lies
I tell myself
more violent
than indifference.

A ship on course
has wide lanes,
but a ship arrived
goes through a narrow passage.

I lost my compass
somewhere in her channels.

I drift with lost ships
and make peace with my betrayals.

18FEB

Tell me,
do you believe in heaven?
Surely it is inside our mothers and fathers.

I never once saw a man or woman
who wasn't both temple and castle.

We build walls to keep out darkness
and altars to invade the endless chasm.

I stop.
Invade the silence.

I leave no rock unturned
until I find balance.

It reads like a scroll
cast out on the ocean.

A secret message
penned in light,
brought through the ages
and to this very moment.

19FEB

The mark is half past the line
on the horizon
and the dark side
of her vast reflected island.

The moon has no light of her own,
only a reflection of a greater glow—
with one side cast in shadow
and the other laid in stone.

You are my light, my love,
I need you to shine.

Where does her light come from?

I didn't give up.
I gave in to silence.

— *s i l e n c e* —

20FEB ♍✒ 🌓

But her color.

Her color!

I can't live without her color.

Her color speaks
a deep and foreign tongue.

I am the artisan.
She is the canvas.

— RED —

She
is too
loud
for me
to *b r e a t h e.*

21FEB ♍♐ 🌓

I feel the space
between my eyes
begin to burn.

My teeth
become numb,
and I lose focus.

I catch my breath
with gasps
like swallowed diamonds,
and violently
I am reminded *what is holy.*

I feel like painting myself
                    r e d
and sketching crosses
across my forehead
and my chest.

I feel the thunder
in my rib cage,
and I am present
in the halls of the abyss.

I can see *nothing*
but her light.

She.

Is.

Too.

B r *i* g h t.

22FEB

"If your eye is single,
your whole body
will be full of light."

— ~~VIOLENT~~ *VIOLET* —

I close both eyes
and plunge into the ruin.

I watch a man
pry water from a hydrant.
Am I that much different
when I'm thirsty in desire?

Surely I am not a tool
but *my own master.*

22FEB

Her hips
unfold into tunnels.

Dear God
be in this space.

23FEB

Free into the place
that brought me—

I search for silence
in the bed sheets,
but I hear only sirens.

I hold my breath.
I draw into a sea
of flame and motion.

Her lips become an island.
Her smile tunes me into focus.

— *sunlight in my eyes* —

I wake up breathless
in a rage of blind devotion.

I had a home!
I was the ocean!

I TEAR HER OFF MY WALLS
WITH MY EMOTIONS.

— *BLACK & BLUE* —

Freedom is a word
with false agreements
painted across each letter
so I'll believe it.

Have you ever wondered
what's in the mind of a man
strung out on nervous pacing?

It is a dungeon.

I can't explain the halls
that lead a mind from love to hate,
but I can see the miles in my shoes.

It stretches a man to endlessly
scan the floor for a silence to the absence
that won't let him rest his head.

— *BLACK* —

I pace restless across my room,
as I gasp to catch my breath.

Eventually my lungs
will grow tired of poison
and give in to *the nothing*—
the body is not a *never ending story*.

I breathe in toxic fumes
then exhale fumes more toxic.

24FEB

It's true no man is an island.
The faithless die many times
before their death.

I pace with God
in sways of hell.
Days become months
and still no rest.

If you ever find yourself at the high gates,
tell the watcher of the bell tower
you've been here too.

Her grief will swell the courts with sorrow
and give you passage into heaven.

"How dark is darkness that even
with light you give up,
and how bright is truth if even
after all this there's still love?

How you walk through the fire
is more important
than where you wind up.
You will burn.
You will not burn up."

I hear it like thunder.

I take up
a different sword.

— once more into the silence —

I sit on my roof
and watch the lightning remind me
that the earth is full of electricity.

I can't shake the feeling
that I am somehow a part of it all.

Every time the sky flashes
I feel more connected.

25FEB ♑ ☽

— lightning —

In waves
of yellow neurons
light connects the earth
to the heavens.

I imagine the clouds
to be my head,
as my thoughts
fire electricity
down my spine,
and I imagine the ground
my body,
as my intention
spirals northward
toward the skyline.

Every time I watch a storm,
it reminds me that my life
is directed by my thoughts—
the electrical impulses
from my head to my body.

In one brilliant moment,
desire can fire
from my head to my feet
then into motion,

i n t e n t i o n,

it seems,
is the most powerful of motivators.

I spent half my life searching,
following the bread crumbs
of some mysterious light,
but it was always calling me,
beckoning me ever closer to its fire.

Every brief moment we connect,
I walk away with more questions
and a greater obsession
with finding it again,
holding on to it for longer
and becoming more congruent
with each photon
in the *boundless light of truth.*

I sit restless with the lightning
and realize the path to clarity
is to stop looking.
I sit still and wait
for the storm inside to unearth me.

26FEB ♄○

Like the first man
to inspect the rings of Saturn,
I analyze the sky
as the sky analyzes me.

Like the first woman
to unearth a mountain spring,
I become a part of the earth
as the earth becomes a part of me.

"Every whim of nature
is a reflection of our divinity,
just as every whim of love
is a reflection of the divine."

I hear it like bells in my left ear.

— deeper into this curious silence —

I stop and cast my eye

                to the sky.

I listen to a timeless story told

by its billion burning suns,

written in the ancient and mysterious tongue

that told its story

to the first eye

to gaze the stars in wonder.

27FEB

With light the ink,
with time the scroll,
with imagination the feeble characters,
I listen with my eye cast
              to the heavens
and stand composed
beneath the silent universe in triumph—
before its billion onlooking messengers
singing ageless songs of light—
for the universe
is one symphony of love and color,
in harmony with
the choirs of heaven.

I see the colors
in this new light's spires.
I know if I stare long enough
the light will meet me

       eye to eye.

— the silence beckons me —

I make space
for nobility and honor,
so that,
with enough time emitting,
I may live long enough
to stand for something eternal,
something profound
that has no other recourse
than to push me to the edge of myself,
that I may embrace a new perspective
and become a noble column
among the rich halls of humanity,
and in this single action,
together,
become one expression of color
painted out across the canvas of time.

I am a cathedral.
A prodigal
of endless chambers.
I enter through holy gates
boundless
like a child,
curious and unreluctant.

I stand in the space between
the narrow gate,
where the light dwells,

as color strides through
the prism in my eye.

I am a cathedral.
I am arches and stained glass.

The vaulted ceiling
in my heart
stretches up
into the cosmos.

It reminds me to
tune my instrument
and temper myself
into whole notes.

I can hear the infinite
echo through the hallways.

In this unhollow *fray*
there is only *Sound*.
There is only *Light*.
There is only *God*.

I was born of light
and cast into darkness,
a member of the race of humans
literally born in the bellies
of suns and stardust,
each an equal heir
in the endless line of *promise*.

How vast is my ocean?

Multiply the circumference of the earth by ten
you have a solar system,
then divide your cells by ten
you have a quantum ecosystem.

I have as many particles in my finger
as stars in our skies.

How could I waste a moment feeling lonely
with *a whole universe inside*?

— indigo —

I once heard a story about a man
who climbed a pillar,
at the center of the
highest hill in Syria.

From his vantage he could see
a line of people walking
willingly off the cliffs into the sea.
At the ledges he could see the kingdom's
towers reaching high above but
hiding in the clouds like cowards.

And so the blind led
the blind into the chasm,
and the faithless led
the faithful into madness.
They say the high altitude
never broke him—,
        v e r t i g o
could shake the
earth but not his focus.

Never doubt that in one day
you can change the world.
Every paradigm that rocked Earth's orbit
first happened in one head
and in one moment.

— blue —

I step into the silence like I mean it.
I stop making arrangements
with my alter ego.

I am clear in the understanding
that this very moment
could change my whole ending.

28FEB

— my right ear becomes a gateway —

The bells!
I hear the bells again!

— the silence becomes an ocean —

I hear a tiny voice
that sounds like clarity.
I follow it like wind
across my salt-filled sea
until I reach the mountains.

Love speaks my name
compelling me to climb higher,
beyond the gateway
to some holy mountain,
and past a spiraling staircase
to the fire.

She is here now too,
but I hear nothing.

— silence inhabits me —

I climb to the top
and step out
onto the rooftop of the world.

From this vantage—
higher than the fog of my desire—
every path that lies in darkness
comes to light.

Don't blink,
the light is getting louder.

Eye to eye.
Light to light.
My hands.
Her sight.

— *the earth spins VIOLEnTly* —

I can see her smile in the mirror.

My vision blurs.

Light diffuses into halos.

I close one eye to focus on the nameless.

White on the feet of the infinite,

a weightless song whispers

in the night of my garden.

"There is nothing she has

that you need."

— *BLUE blue* —

FEET.

The
portal
is in
my
feet.

Kēys hide beneath them.

I reach into the silence
with legs as
tall as steeples.
I give in to the roots beneath me
and find shelter in my weakness.

I grow tall like a seed
stretched into spires and then fruit.
I draw into the secret—
the unfleeting *boundless blue*.

I can only see the color of silence,
and through my leaves
I hear she's gone.

1MAR

♓ ○

Vertigo is letting go.
Silence is like *vertigo*.

I
can
breathe
now.

I remember *blue* and nothing,
a heavenly distortion.
My roots in whirling wind.

I could not know the warmth
of the amber afterglow,
nor the *Light* that does not know darkness.

wellsprings

Fire is a *boundless birth*
mingled in precious metal.

I hear it over and over in my head
as I fall asleep.

— 11:11 —

With love the only gold,
I followed each golden step
until I reached the moon.

I left a light on in the wild.

The moon cast her clothes
off onto the world—
like a bride's dress
she would wear only once—
and draped my eyes
in fresh new linen.

I rang fourteen bells of hope
to prove I was alive.

I followed the footsteps
of the nameless.

I was the lightning
that strikes relentless.

I unveiled twenty-two lampstands
until I cast no shadow.

Then,
I stop.

I close one eye to focus.

I open the vault
of the weightless,
and read a book
to stir my mind.

I write thirty-three proofs
that love is real—
painting each theorem
a mirror of the other—
proving hope the ship,
faith the wind,
and love the golden anchor.

Light becomes a flame unsettled.
It rattles cage after cage—
a heavy wave cast against the current.

A golden voice
crashes against my hollow vessel
in the moment.

"Wē are the ocean."

Before a face was—
before knowledge took form—
Lovē filled.

vērtigo

AN OPEN LETTER TO THE LOST

O'Lost,

We are a lost generation of analog people living in a digital age, where truth has gone the alternative way of rumor, social good has become secondary to economic gain, beauty is defined by Photoshop, and prejudice has become the dominate voice of our generation. The silicon age of information has smothered us into paralysis, stolen our privacy, and conditioned us to line up to be the first to buy big brother.

The world has never needed voices of resistance more, voices of hope and self-love, of fresh water and empowerment. We desperately need more Bob Dylan and Maya Angelou style voices. Join us and commit your art to the resistance. Great art has purpose . . .

Sincerely from the planet Earth,

Analog de Lēon
A Moniker of Chris Purifoy

Join the resistance at *lostpoets.org.*

A few guidelines for a healthier Earth—
(1) No hate. (2) Be love. (3) Resist injustice.

APPENDIX

1. Page x. *"Anam Cara"*
    Gaelic for "soul mate," and also the title of a book by John O'Donohue.

2. Page x. *"She is an idea that could launch a thousand ships."*
    An allusion to Helen of Troy.

3. Page 1, 4, 117. *"Rooftop of the world"*
    An allusion to Walt Whitman's "Song of Myself."

4. Page 19. *"I once heard the most beautiful / of all creations lives in the shadow / of a candle on a cave wall."*
    An allusion to a passage from the book *Anam Cara* by John O'Donohue.

5. Pages 24–25. *Illustration Spread 1.*
    The sky in this spread samples *Starry Night Over the Rhône* by Vincent van Gogh.

6. Page 26. *"Sing in me, Muse."*
    The opening to *The Odyssey* by Homer.

7. Page 29. *"Ouroboros"*
    An ancient symbol depicting a serpent or dragon eating its own tail, meant to denote a continuous cycle or infinity.

8. Page 29. *"She flees from me like Orion, / a great huntress afraid of scorpions."*
    An allusion to the story of Orion in Greek mythology. Orion died from a scorpion sting, and so the constellation Scorpio rises on one side of the sky as Orion sinks across the opposite horizon, a symbolic Orion running away from the scorpion across the skies forever.

9. Page 36. *"Odysseus"*
    The king of Ithaca and central figure of *The Odyssey*.

10. Page 38. *"I drink from the pool of memory, / so I will remember . . ."*
    An allusion to the spring of Mnemosyne from Greek mythology. Initiates would drink from the spring of Mnemosyne, the pool of memory, which would stop the transmigration of the soul.

11. Page 39. *"No one tells you / when you fall in love with a star, / one day it might burn out / and leave behind a black hole."*
An allusion to astrophysics, specifically referencing the relationship between supernovas and black holes. A supernova occurs when a star's core collapses, causing a violent explosion of the outer layers of the star, but if the star has enough energy, it may also collapse further and form a black hole.

12. Page 40. *"— the arrow of time moves forward —"*
An allusion to physics and the nature of time, often referred to as a forward-moving arrow that moves in only one direction, or asymmetry of time. The "arrow of time" occurs because of the second law of thermodynamics.

13. Pages 42–43. *Illustration Spread 2.*
The sky in this spread samples *The Starry Night* by Vincent van Gogh.

14. Page 48. *"Narrow passage"*
An allusion to a verse from the Bible, Matthew 7:13. "Enter through the narrow gate. For wide is the gate and broad is the road that leads to destruction, and many enter through it."

15. Page 54. *"The mark"*
An allusion to a Greek term mentioned in the Bible and in *The Iliad* by Homer, "hamartano" (αμαρτανω). It means "to miss the mark," and was later translated to the English word "sin."

16. Page 66. *"If your eye is single, / your whole body / will be full of light."*
Referring to a quote by Jesus from the Bible, Matthew 6:22.

17. Page 79. *". . . and give in to the nothing— / the body is not a never ending story."*
References to the movie, *The NeverEnding Story*. "The nothing" refers to the dark storm that was engulfing the fictional world of Fantasia, in the film and book, *The NeverEnding Story*.

18. Page 81. *"It's true no man is an island."*
An allusion to John Donne's "XVII. Meditation" from *Devotions upon Emergent Occasions and severall steps in my Sicknes*, 1624.

19. Page 82. *"How you walk through the fire / is more important / than where you wind up."*
An allusion to *What Matters Most Is How Well You Walk Through the Fire*, a book by Charles Bukowski.

20. Page 84. "— *once more into the silence* —"
An allusion to Shakespeare's *Henry V*, "Once more unto the breach, dear friends, once more . . . "

21. Page 102. "*as color strides through / the prism in my eye.*"
An allusion to optics, and the way a transparent triangular prism refracts light into color, and the way the eye translates light reflections into color.

22. Page 103. "*It reminds me to / tune my instrument / and temper myself / into whole notes.*"
An allusion to the dual definitions for the word "temperament."
1. A person or animal's nature, especially as it permanently affects their behavior.
2. The adjustment of intervals in tuning a piano or other musical instrument so as to fit the scale.

23. Page 104. " . . . *literally born in the bellies / of suns and stardust,*"
An allusion to physics, specifically the fusion force of nature, as the means for the creation of all matter and energy inside of burning stars.

24. Page 105. "*Multiply the circumference of the earth by ten / you have a solar system, / then divide your cells by ten / you have a quantum ecosystem.*"
An allusion to the theories of quantum mechanics and relativity. The reference speaks to the nature of the many orders of magnification, or magnitude, as a means to connect the smallest particles, humans, the planets, and the stars, into one unified system.

25. Page 105. "*How could I waste a moment feeling lonely / with a whole universe inside?*"
An allusion to "In Your Light," a poem by Jalāl ad-Dīn Muhammad Rūmī, a 13th-century Persian poet, scholar, and sufi mystic.

26. Page 106. "*I once heard a story about a man / who climbed a pillar, / at the center of the / highest hill in Syria.*"
a) An allusion to St. Simeon Stylites, a Syriac ascetic saint who achieved notability for living thirty-six years on a small platform on top of a pillar near Aleppo (in modern Syria). He lived there as a symbol for resistance to problems with his culture, and he started a movement. Many more pillar protestors would follow his lead throughout the next few hundred years.
b) "St Simeon Stylites" is also a poem written by Alfred Tennyson in 1833 and published in his 1842 collection of poetry.

27. Page 106. *"And so the blind led / the blind into the chasm, / and the faithless led / the faithful into madness."*

    An allusion to *King Lear* by Shakespeare: "'Tis the time's plague when madmen lead the blind."

28. Pages 107–109. *Illustration Spread 3.*

    This spread features Aleppo, a central city in Syria, before the bombings from recent wars that have left it desolate. It also features St. Simeon Stylites, a 12th-century Syrian monk who lived atop a pillar in Syria in protest to the darkness of the day. Millions of people have lost their homes, their families, and their lives in Syria. Let us never forget them.

29. Page 114. *"... across my salt-filled sea"*

    An allusion to science, but also a speech by John F. Kennedy: "It is an interesting biological fact that all of us have in our veins the exact same percentage of salt in our blood that exists in the ocean, and, therefore, we have salt in our blood, in our sweat, in our tears. We are tied to the ocean."

30. Page 114. *"... beyond the gateway / to some holy mountain,"*

    An allusion to the book, *Mount Analogue* by René Daumal. This book is one of Analog's largest literary influences.

31. Page 114. *"... and past a spiraling staircase"*

    An allusion to the winding staircase in Freemasonry legend.

32. Page 114. *"... the fire."*

    An allusion to the burning bush and fiery cloud in the legend of Moses from the Bible (Exodus 3 and 24).

33. Pages 121, 129. *"I / can / breathe / now." "There is nothing she has / that you need."*

    Allusions to U2's twelfth studio album, *No Line on the Horizon*, one of the major inspirations for *Vertigo* and Analog's favorite record.

34. Page 142. *"... a heavy wave cast against the current."*

    An allusion to the closing lines of *The Great Gatsby*, by F. Scott Fitzgerald.

Fiorella Giordano,

Thank you for your endless creativity and support as this book matured. My favorite lines are filled with your voice and your boundlessness. Your infinite vision filled the roots of this book with wind and mystery. Without you, this book could never have been. Higher still . . .

Gabriel Sage,

Your creativity is a vast expanse. Thank you for being real
with me. Your influence grounded this book and saved it
from obscurity. You helped me unpack its ideas in a way I
never could have done without you. O'Lost, O'Found.

ABOUT THE AUTHOR

Analog de Lēon is a moniker by Chris Purifoy. Chris is a writer, technology architect, and futurist. He speaks in global forums about the slippery slope of progress and the importance of art with purpose. Analog is an initiative to encourage people to unplug and be present in their lives.

Read Chris's full bio at *goingvertigo.com/bio*.